CIVICS

Liz Brown

WEIGL PUBLISHERS INC.

Published by Weigl Publishers Inc.
350 5th Avenue, Suite 3304, PMB 6G
New York, NY 10118-0069

Website: www.weigl.com
Copyright ©2008 WEIGL PUBLISHERS INC.

All of the Internet URLs given in the book were valid at the time of publication. However, due to the dynamic nature of the Internet, some addresses may have changed, or sites may have ceased to exist since publication. While the author and publisher regret any inconvenience this may cause readers, no responsibility for any such changes can be accepted by either the author or the publisher.

Library of Congress Cataloging-in-Publication Data

Brown, Liz (Elizabeth A.)
  Civics / Liz Brown.
      p. cm. -- (Social studies essential skills)
  Includes index.
  ISBN 978-1-59036-765-0 (lib. bdg. : alk. paper) -- ISBN 978-1-59036-766-7 (soft cover : alk. paper)
  1. Citizenship--United States--Juvenile literature. 2. Civics--Juvenile literature. I. Title.
  JK1759.B886 2008
  320.473--dc22

                                 2007024012

Printed in the United States of America
1 2 3 4 5 6 7 8 9 0 11 10 09 08 07

Editor: Heather C. Hudak
Design: Terry Paulhus

Every reasonable effort has been made to trace ownership and to obtain permission to reprint copyright material. The publishers would be pleased to have any errors or omissions brought to their attention so that they may be corrected in subsequent printings.

Table of Contents

What is Civics?

Civics is the study of the rights and duties that come with being a member of a country. Members of a country are called citizens. A citizen is a person who lives in a given place and has relationships with other people in that place.

Citizenship refers to the laws of a place or the shared **values**, traditions, and beliefs of the people who live there. Citizens of the United States have many personal freedoms that are protected by the **Bill of Rights**. These rights give people the freedom to speak their opinion, practice different religions, and be treated equally by others.

People's values and beliefs may change over time. If they are active in their community, they can change the community to reflect their values and beliefs.

When citizens are very active, they learn a great deal about events and issues that affect their community. They take part in decision-making activities. Active citizens try to influence others to share their beliefs. Can you think of any ways you or your family play an active role in your community?

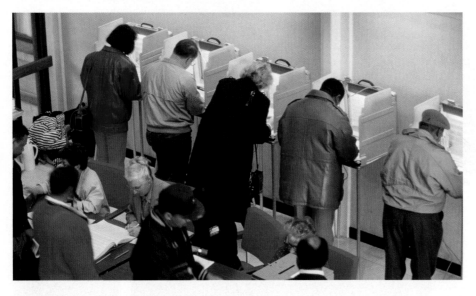

Voting is a decision-making activity.

Taking Part in the Community

To be an active citizen, a person should try to help fulfill community needs. Becoming a team coach, helping build a fence at the school, and helping someone carry their groceries are examples of filling needs. Sometimes, the community needs to work together to reach a goal. One group of citizens may want to build a road where another group wants to build a playground. Active citizens voice their opinions and help convince others to agree with them. Read the case study about how one family helped its community.

One summer, a farmer decided to grow a new crop of vegetables. In autumn, he was not able to sell the entire crop to stores. He donated the leftover vegetables to a local food bank. The next year, the farmer's children wanted to help the community. They decided to grow their own crop for the food bank. The children spent the summer tending to their crop. They watered and weeded the fields. When the crop was ready to harvest, the food bank sent volunteers to help pick the vegetables. Many citizens worked together to help provide food for people who could not afford to buy it.

Thinking about what you have read, talk about these questions with a friend. Why would the farmer's children want to spend their summer growing a crop? How did this help fill a need in their community? What special resources did they have? What resources do you have? How could you or your family help the community?

What is Decision Making?

Decision making is one of the main tasks of citizenship. Citizens make decisions on their own or as part of a group. These decisions can affect all of the citizens living in a certain place.

There are many ways to make decisions. Basic decisions are those citizens make on their own. People who make good decisions often have a plan for making decisions. They may begin by thinking about or identifying the problem. Then, they gather and organize information about the problem. Next, they think about solutions, make a choice, and take action.

Sometimes, a group of people needs to make decisions together. These people may have different beliefs or opinions. They may try to convince others in the group to see the problem from another **perspective**. They hope to influence the group's decision.

The United States is a **democracy**. In a democracy, people work together to make important decisions about the country. There may be a democracy at work in your school, in the form of a student **government**, or council. Have you had to work in a group to make a decision? How did you work together? Did some people try to convince others to see a different perspective?

A citizen who builds a compost heap in her backyard has made a decision about waste removal in her community.

Making Decisions in a Democracy

In a school government, a group of students is elected to make decisions that affect the student body. The people in the group must be aware of the different needs and views of the student body in order to make decisions that are fair. Read the case study about a student council that needs to make a fair decision. Then, answer the questions.

Sarah is president of the student council at her school. Other students voted for her during a school election. As president, she must lead the student council as it makes decisions for the other students at the school. The teachers have given the student council $1,000 to spend on items for the students. The student council must decide what is most needed and wanted by the students in the school. Some students want to have a dance. All students at the school could attend the dance. The football team wants new jerseys because the old jerseys are very worn. The band would like to buy instruments so students do not have to provide their own.

Make a list of things you would want the student council to spend the money on. How can Sarah and the rest of the student council make a decision that is fair? What steps can they take to be sure they make a good decision?

What are Rules and Laws?

Most decisions that you make are influenced by rules and laws. Rules tell a person how he or she should act. Rules are made to protect people and promote the **common good**.

Families often have rules, such as a limiting the amount of television that can be watched. Schools and classrooms also have rules. Most classrooms have rules about doing homework, being late to class, and how to treat others. If these rules are not followed, there are **consequences**.

Laws are rules that are made by the government. Just like rules, laws are made to protect people and promote the common good. Everyone must obey these laws. There are laws about many things, including driving cars, stealing, and hurting others. If people break the law, they may have to pay a fine. If the person commits a serious crime, he or she may be arrested and put in jail.

*Most groups have rules that their members must follow. The House of Representatives, the part of the **federal** government that proposes and votes on laws, has a long list of rules. In the house, there are rules for beginning and ending a session, and rules for speaking. Some of these rules may be similar to the rules of your classroom.*

Evaluating the Law

When laws are made, some people may lose rights and freedoms, while others may gain rights and freedoms. Read the case study about how a new law took away some people's rights but helped others.

A community created a law that banned people from skateboarding on the sidewalks. Skateboarding was only permitted in special parks. Skateboarders who did not obey the law would lose the right to skateboard in any part of the community for up to one year. People who did not skateboard gained the right to walk safely on the sidewalk.

Take a look at the laws below. Decide who would lose freedoms and who would gain freedoms in places that have these laws.

A law is made that bans smoking in all public places.

A new law requires dog owners to always have their dogs on leashes in the park.

Authority and Power

Part of citizenship is understanding how the government works. To take part in the decision-making process, citizens must know about the structures and procedures of the government.

The government has the **authority** to make and enforce the laws of the United States. Citizens have given the government this power through an **election**. Citizens can take part in an election by learning about the people who are running for government. They vote for the person they think will do the job best. Some citizens may take part by running for office.

Teachers have the authority to make rules in a classroom. This power is given to them by parents and the school. Sometimes, people who do not have authority try to use power to make others follow their orders. A school bully may use fear to force others to do something. The bully is not allowed to do this because it interferes with other students' freedoms.

Police officers have the power to direct traffic or hand out tickets to lawbreakers. Are there any times when you have power or authority?

Assessing Power and Authority

Read the paragraph about a time in history when Great Britain had control of the American colonies. Then, answer the questions.

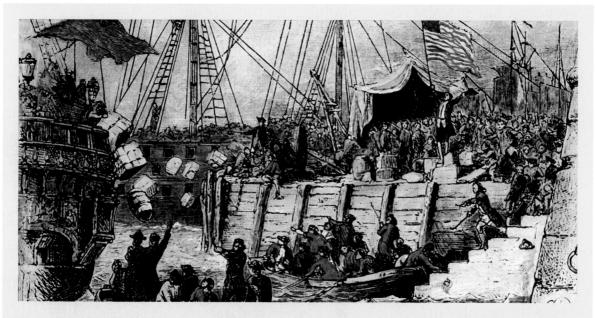

In 1773, Great Britain had control over the American colonies. This gave Great Britain the authority to make decisions for the colonies. The British **Parliament** passed the Tea Act. It allowed a ship from the East India Co. to sell tea to the American colonies for a cheaper price than the people who sold tea and lived in the colonies. American colonists were unhappy.

To **protest** the Tea Act, the people in Boston would not allow a ship from the East India Co. to unload its cargo of tea. On December 16, 1773, a group of men boarded the boat and dumped the tea into the Boston Harbor. This was known as the Boston Tea Party.

1. Did Great Britain have the power and authority to make decisions for the American Colonies?
2. How did the people of Boston try to influence Great Britain's decision?

The Government

A government makes it possible for people to work together to achieve goals they could not reach if they worked alone. In the United States, there are three levels of government. They are the local, state, and federal government. Each level of government has different responsibilities, but they are all linked in important ways.

One of the main duties of government is to create and enforce laws. However, governments do many other things. Governments collect **taxes**. The money collected provides services to citizens. Governments also provide sanitation services, such as garbage disposal. They maintain a military that protects the country in times of war.

Roads and schools are built using tax money.

Writing a Letter

People can influence the government. They can vote, protest, and write letters. This case study shows how one person influenced the government.

Rosa Parks, an African American woman, influenced the U.S. government by refusing to give up her seat on a bus in Montgomery, Alabama, in 1955. At this time, African Americans were not allowed to sit in the same seats as other bus riders. Rosa was arrested for not giving up her seat. Many African Americans protested by not riding the buses in the city of Montgomery. This led to a decision to allow African Americans to sit with the other riders on the bus. Rosa Parks' act of protest helped influence the government.

You can influence the government, too. Write a letter to a person in government about something that concerns you. It could be a letter about the law, environment, or any other issue that you feel is important.

The Constitution

When creating laws in the United States, governments must follow the laws of the Constitution. The Constitution is a document that describes how the government works and explains the rights and freedoms of American citizens.

The Constitution is more powerful than the government. If a government does something that opposes the Constitution, it can be declared **unconstitutional**.

The Constitution can be **amended**. This does not happen often. Thousands of amendments have been proposed. However, only 27 amendments have been made since the Constitution was written in 1787.

The 13th amendment was made to the Constitution in 1865. This amendment banned slavery in the United States. At the time, not all of the southern states approved this amendment. Today, all states have approved the 13th amendment.

The 22nd amendment to the Constitution limits the president to serving no more than two terms. This amendment was passed in 1947, following President Franklin Delano Roosevelt's death. Roosevelt was the first president to serve more than two terms.

Protected versus Unprotected Speech

Read this paragraph about the Bill of Rights.

*The Founding Fathers of the United States wanted their country to be democratic and fair. They wrote a Bill of Rights into the Constitution. The Bill of Rights includes the First Amendment. It guarantees the freedom of speech and the right to have peaceable assembly. This means that people can voice their opinions and protest things they do not believe are fair. However, there are some instances where speech is not protected. The freedom of speech can be limited to protect the privacy and rights of others. Some examples of unprotected speech include words that may incite violence or put national security at risk, and false or **defamatory** statements that are printed by a newspaper.*

Visit **www.ncac.org**, and type in "protected speech" and "unprotected speech" to learn more. Then, see if you can tell which of these examples are protected or unprotected speech.

A newspaper publishes an untrue story about the mayor of your town.

A person writes a letter to the governor of his state to say he is angry about a new law.

A group of people march in front of the White House to protest a war.

The leader of a protest makes a speech, telling people to break windows and steal.

Local Government

The local government looks after and serves the needs of the people in your community. County and **municipal** governments are found at the local level. These governments take care of public safety, city streets, parks, trash removal, and other services that a town or city needs to run efficiently.

Towns and cities are run by elected officials. In most town or city governments, there is a mayor and a council. Council members represent different wards, or areas of a city. The mayor is the head of the council. The mayor and council propose and vote on decisions that influence the way that the town or city is run.

Municipal governments often meet to make decisions at a town or city hall.

New York City's City Hall is one of the oldest in the United States. It was built between 1803 and 1812. Inside is the Governor's Room. It holds many artifacts that tell the history of New York and the United States. Important people, such as Albert Einstein and Abraham Lincoln, have visited the Governor's Room.

Helping to Solve a Community Problem

Every community has problems that the local government tries to solve. The problems may include litter in parks, homelessness, or theft. Citizens in the community can also help solve these problems through volunteering. Volunteers can help by cleaning up the litter in a park, collecting food for a charity, or organizing a club that watches over the neighborhood. Many groups work to improve communities. This paragraph is about one of these groups.

Interact is a service club for students 14 to 18 years old. These clubs are run in many high schools throughout the United States. Each year, Interact clubs organize different community service projects. One project involved raising money to provide school supplies for Afghan children. Projects such as this help build leadership skills, respect for others, and a sense of goodwill.

Community service projects can include collecting money for a charity or cleaning up trash. Think about a problem in your community. Are there any ways that you can help solve the problem?

State Government

The state government looks after the state in which you live. There are three branches of government at the state level. These are the executive branch, the judicial branch, and the legislative branch. The leader of the executive branch is called the governor. The governor is a state's representative before national and international governments.

The state government has many duties. It sets standards for schools and provides money for public education. The state government manages health care, housing, and welfare programs for people who are in need of help. It builds and maintains state highways and protects the safety of the people through the state National Guard. The state National Guard is part of the United States Army. It assists people during emergencies, such as floods and earthquakes.

Each state has its own constitution. States must abide by the rules of their constitution, as well as the rules of the U.S. Constitution. In order to make sure state governments do not have too much power, they must list all limits on their power in their state constitutions. Each rule or **clause** *in a state constitution must be explained in detail.*

Locating State Capitals

The government of each state is located in the state capital. This is the place where the government of the state meets. What is the name of your state capital? The locations of ten state capitals are marked on the map below. Can you name each capital and the state in which it is located?

Answers: 1.) Providence, Rhode Island 2.) Albany, New York 3.) Harrisburg, Pennsylvania 4.) Annapolis, Maryland 5.) Columbus, Ohio 6.) Hartford, Connecticut 7.) Dover, Delaware 8.) Boston, Massachusetts 9.) Trenton, New Jersey 10.) Augusta, Maine

Federal Government

The federal government looks after the entire country. It is responsible for creating money, regulating trade, communicating with other countries, and providing national defense. Like state governments, the federal government has three branches—the executive, legislative, and judicial.

The legislative branch includes Congress and other government agencies. Congress consists of the House of Representatives and the Senate. They propose and pass laws for the United States.

The executive branch consists of the president, vice president, and cabinet. It ensures that the laws of the United States are obeyed. The president approves laws that are created by Congress. The president also can veto, or reject, a law.

The judicial branch passes judgment on court cases that have to do with federal law. It consists of the Supreme Court and lower federal courts.

There is a separation of powers between the three branches of the federal government. Each branch has its own responsibilities, but they all work together to run the country. Any of the three branches may use its power to check the powers of the other branches. This is called a system of checks and balances. It ensures that no one branch has too much power. For example, if Congress approves a law, the president can veto it if he does not agree.

Identifying Government Branches

There are many important buildings in the nation's capital, Washington, D.C. Select one of the buildings from the pictures on this page. Research online to find out what branch of government works in this building. What are the responsibilities of this branch? Write a paragraph that describes what it does.

The Capitol

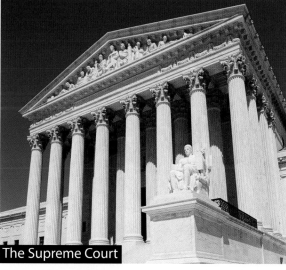

The Supreme Court

The White House

Putting Your Knowledge To Use

Governments create laws, protect people, and allow citizens to work together to accomplish things they could not accomplish alone. Test your knowledge about the systems of government in the United States.

1. What is civics?

2. What is the Constitution?

3. What are the three levels of government?

4. How can citizens influence the government?

5. What are the three branches of government at the state and federal levels?

Answers:

1. Civics is the study of the rights and duties that come with being a member of a country.

2. The Constitution is a document that describes how the government works and explains the rights and freedoms of American citizens.

3. The three levels of government are federal, state, and local.

4. Citizens can influence the government through voting, protesting, and writing letters.

5. The three branches of government are legislative, executive, and judicial.

Websites for Further Research

Many books and websites provide information on civics and the government. To learn more about the government, borrow books from the library, or surf the Internet.

To find out more about civics and the government, type key words, such as "United States government," into the search field of your Web browser.

Learn more about how the government works. Visit *Ben's Guide to U.S. Government For Kids* at *http://bensguide.gpo.gov*

Find out more about the U. S. Constitution at *www.usconstitution.net/constkidsK.html*

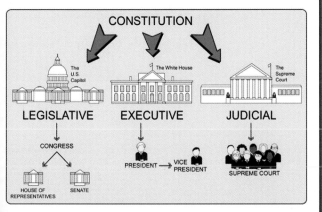

Branches of Government

CONSTITUTION

The U.S. Capitol — The White House — The Supreme Court

LEGISLATIVE — **EXECUTIVE** — **JUDICIAL**

CONGRESS — PRESIDENT → VICE PRESIDENT — SUPREME COURT

HOUSE OF REPRESENTATIVES — SENATE

The Founding Fathers, the framers of the Constitution, wanted to form a government that did not allow one person to have too much authority or control. While under the rule of the British they learned that this could be a bad system. Yet government under the Articles of Confederation taught them that there was a need for a strong centralized government.

With this in mind the framers wrote the Constitution to provide for a separation of powers, or three separate branches of government. Each has its own responsibilities and at the same time they work together to make the country run smoothly and to assure that the rights of citizens are not ignored or disallowed. This is done through checks and balances. A branch may use its powers to check the powers of the other two in order to maintain a balance of power among the three branches of government.

The three branches of the U.S. Government are the legislative, executive, and judicial. A complete diagram of the branches of the U.S. Government may be found in the U.S. Government Manual (PDF).

To learn more, choose from the following:

- *Branches of Government*
- Legislative Branch
- Executive Branch
- Judicial Branch

The Constitution for Kids

This file is intended for students in Kindergarten through 3rd grade. Other versions of this page are available:

- The Constitution for Kids: 4th through 7th Grade
- The Constitution for Kids: 8th through 12th Grade
- Pictures of the Constitution
- The main site

If you have any questions about any words or ideas on this page, please ask your parents or teachers for help. Understanding the Constitution is important for all Americans, even kids!

If there is anything that could be improved on this page, please let The Webmaster know!

Want to see pictures of the Constitution, or to find coloring pages for you to color yourself? Click here!

The Basics

The law is the set of rules that we live by. The Constitution is the highest law. It belongs to the United States. It belongs to all Americans.

The Constitution says how the government works. It creates the President. It creates the Congress. It creates the Supreme Court.

The Constitution lists some key rights. Rights are things that all people have just because they are alive. By listing the rights, they are made special. They are made safe. The Bill of Rights is a part of the Constitution. The Bill of Rights lists many rights of the people.

Glossary

amended: made changes to a document

authority: having the power to make rules and decisions

Bill of Rights: a written document that outlines the freedoms of Americans

clause: a section, provision, or article of a document

common good: something that is beneficial to all members of a society

consequences: the results of actions

defamatory: something that damages a person's reputation

democracy: a system of government in which all people are able to run for a position of leadership and vote for their representatives

election: the process of choosing a government

federal: a central system of government for the entire country

government: an organization that makes rules and takes care of a school, town, state, or country

municipal: relating to a town or city

parliament: the highest level of a governing body

perspective: point of view or attitude toward something

protest: objection to something

taxes: money that workers contribute to the government to help pay for roads, schools, and other services

unconstitutional: against the Constitution

values: principles that are thought to be important

Index